I said... I'm not done feeling yet

Ta'ziana Zhane

BookLeaf Publishing

India | USA | UK

Presentation by *BookLeaf Publishing*

Web: www.bookleafpub.com

E-mail: info@bookleafpub.com

ISBN: 9789357444545

First edition 2022

DEDICATION

I dedicate this book to myself.

To the little girl who thought her dreams were too far to ever reach. To the little girl with a tender heart and big feelings.

The little girl who just wanted something more for herself.

She never knew how she would do it; she only knew she had to.

To the little girl who had so much fucking resilience.

To the woman who never stops crying.

To the woman that inspires herself over and over and over again.

The woman that always gets back up no matter how long she's down, or how low she feels.

To the woman who has dedicated herself to her healing journey.

To the woman who is stepping into her power.

I made it farther than I ever thought I would and I am so eternally grateful.

To me, because I love myself more than I ever have.

To me, who will continue learning.

And to Ta'ziana, who certainly is not done feeling yet.

This is only the beginning.

ACKNOWLEDGEMENT

I would like to thank my friends. They have supported me so much throughout this journey; I wouldn't be where I am without their wisdom and guidance.

Especially my best friend Sienna, who has seen me through so much over the past ten years. She has always encouraged me to follow my dreams. She believed in me before I knew how to believe in myself.

Thank you again to my friends from the bottom of my heart. I love you all so much.

I am so proud of this body of work; they helped make it possible.

Last thanks go to the Universe and my spiritual team for all of the divine love & guidance.

PREFACE

This poetry is heavily inspired by my own
journey of healing and the lessons I am learning

Pay attention to the lessons

Things change when you decide that you
deserve some of the love that you give to others
When you start getting to know you because
you've never known you
You only knew what was told to you
By the ones who wanted to control you

And the thing is… when you decide to put
yourself first it will make people uncomfortable
So pay attention
The ones who are not for you will reveal
themselves
Watch and listen
Pay attention
Trust your intuition
And the universe will grant your wishes

It will hurt and remember you can't hold your
hurt and theirs
So hold yours and allow other people figure it
out for themselves.

pieces

where am i?
i'm trying to find me
have you seen me?
i feel lost and broken and…
where am i?
am i in pieces?
i don't recognize these pieces
where is the rest of me?
i can't see anything
please tell me if you see me
and please tell me that i miss me
i haven't seen her in ages
who is she?
i mean she is me but i don't feel like me
are you sure this is me?
i mean… am i sure this is me?
please tell me that i miss me
please tell her
i will keep looking for her in these pieces
these pieces of me

capacity for love

i used to think that
knowing deep pain
had ruined me
and made me damaged goods
but it has allowed me
to open my heart
and access the deep reserves of my love

credit

i think i over-identified with being yours
like it somehow contributed more to who i am
than i did
i gave you too much credit
you did not make me amazing or magickal
you did not reach into the depths of my broken
self to retrieve me from the shell i was in
so how is it
i applaud you for the work i did

my normal seasons

i am learning to accept
that my normal
does not look like anyone else's normal
my normal is coping with complex PTSD
and sometimes i feel so alienated that i wish
i wish my normal could be something else

because there are so many days
where simply existing
is so
hard
and so
exhausting

when the nightmares won't stop
and the tears won't stop
when i can't eat
or sleep
when i don't want to get out of bed because i
wake up feeling like i'm about to have an
anxiety attack

it feels like i have more seasons than there are in
a year

sometimes i'll have months that are full of hard
days
and sometimes i can access all the happiness
i'll feel lighter…
but then things get rough again

the truth i often forget about
is that
there is always light in the dark
i just have to be willing to search for it

about me

i have spent an unbelievable amount of time
hating everything about myself
shaming myself
and blaming myself
i don't like the way this feels
so i'm done criticizing
and fantasizing
about how amazing i'd be if i would just fix x, y,
and z

everything about me does not have to be so
awful
though i make it so when i fuel that story
i am amazing right now in this moment
this will be my new story
a story of self-acceptance
in essence

PEDESTAL

you had no business being up there
way up there on that pedestal
on my pedestal
but i gave it to you
i gave it to you because i thought the world of
you
at some point
i decided that you were better than i was
that you were worth more
simply put, i was wrong
granted … i had been pawning off my pedestal
long before i met you
by the time i got to you i had already proven to
be exemplary when it came to putting others
needs before my own
my mother taught me well- ensuring that i would
hear her voice before my own in any
circumstance
for a long time, i didn't know how to turn the
volume down on that
deafening
damaging
debilitating
voice
that i had the most difficult time dismantling

not worth it

sometimes i wish i could fall apart and stay that
way
but i know how hard it is to put myself back
together
so i don't
i've always stayed strong though
and it's wearing on me

hard truths

i know you want desperately for them to really
know what you're feeling
but they can't
maybe no one can
you feel to a degree that they might not
understand
but that's okay
you don't need them to understand
you know
and i know
that what you feel is real
and that your pain is real

fools gold
inconveniences

i would never want to inconvenience you the
way that i've been inconvenienced
and it took me a while to figure out that it was
you
it was you that was inconveniencing me
i thought that it was me
i couldn't even see beyond the fog that danced
around you like it was trying to hide something
like it was trying to make you look better
it made you shine

i blamed myself because i should have known...
you were way too shiny and i loved you way too
blindly
i just want it all behind me
how was i to know
you could put on such a great show
maybe i will always feel foolish and maybe you
will always be clueless
all i know is what my truth is and the truth is i
won't be mistaken

empty

i used to feel like i had this gaping hole in my
chest
where my parents' love should have been
it was so empty
and it made me feel so empty
like i had absolutely nothing to offer
the pain i felt with the absence of my parents'
love was unprecedented
i thought it would kill me
panic attack after panic attack
the pain was consuming me
how could i alone
ever be enough
to fill this void

anymore

i don't cry about you as frequently anymore
i never thought that would happen
and maybe it's just because i have shed so many
tears over you and i know
i know that crying isn't going to bring you back
(i wouldn't want it to)
i know that crying won't change the past
i've cried too much and unfortunately crying
won't fix it
crying won't
make you realize the damage you did to me
when i was the most vulnerable i had ever been
with you
crying didn't
persuade you to treat me better
it didn't
keep you from falling out of love with me
suddenly -
i didn't know you   and
i don't think i ever did
 see
the woman that i fell in love with wouldn't have
said those things to me
she wouldn't have left me
feeling

feeling everything for the both of us
i tried to grab ahold of us
          for us
remember when we said we wouldn't give up on
us
all of those empty prom- us- ses
where did they go

and what did you really mean when you told me
you loved me
and what did you really mean when you said i
was broken
did you really mean that you were broken and so
you had to give up on loving me
suddenly -

i'm not saying i never cry over you anymore
it just doesn't take up most of my time anymore
and you can't leave me at home anymore
in our bed alone anymore
sobbing anymore
longing for the love of my life anymore
because she isn't in my life anymore

i watched her walk out the door
emotionally, mentally, and then physically
you were done before i knew you were done
and we were done before i knew we were done

and is that what you meant when you said you
were over this shit
had enough of this shit
couldn't take any more of my shit
i deserved so much more than that shit
no longer willing to take any more shit from
those who lie about loving me
                see
you may have taught me a few things
but i cannot give you credit anymore
for the work of art that i am anymore
i loved myself into existence
and what do you know about that?
just admit you weren't willing to put in the work
anymore

concept of me

did you really love me
or did you just love the idea of me
the concept of me
but the reality was that i was anxious, broken,
and traumatized wasn't it?
and that wasn't nearly as appealing

afraid to let you choose me

i asked myself why i kept trying so hard
why i kept trying to pour love into you
even though
my cup was so empty   and
it was never enough for you
but there i was
crying into my cup so i'd have something to
pour into yours

i couldn't stop giving to you
when
you couldn't give to me at all
and i was so afraid to let you choose me
because i didn't think you would
or could
and honestly
i'm glad you didn't
you didn't deserve me anyways
and i will never
be that disrespectful to myself again

i thought i deserved you

and all the pain your "love" caused me
little did i know
i am more than worthy of a love that doesn't
cause me pain

us no longer

we will live forever throughout these journal
pages
everything i've tried to forget
it will be here
in this closed journal because
the memory of you is still too painful to touch

how much do you think it breaks my heart that
i cannot have you around
i hate you
because even after everything i know i will
always love you so deeply
i hate you
because i cannot love you anymore
your love took things away from me
love is not supposed to take

just me

what do i do when it's just me
sitting alone
with all this pain
a gaping hole in my chest
chronic loneliness
and no hope in my heart

my soul is being shredded and no one can see it
how do i begin to explain
the depth of my pain

i sob
my body shakes
my heart aches
this ache
makes me want to rip my chest open to relieve
some of the pressure
i wonder how much more of this i can take

missing you//between you and me

my heart is bursting
poems whirr through my head
sweet nothings that barely have any substance
but they are steeped in her
i want to be all yours if you'll have me
-

how do i explain this thing between you and me
when i feel as though it exceeds my body
i want to know where we go when we're that
close
when it's just you and me
and then it's we…
and then it's us
no longer bound by the human in us
when we're like this i feel like stardust
i no longer feel like i am here
i feel like i am there
you know…
there

where the stardust and light are
where the lives before life are

tender-hearted black girl

dear little me
i know your heart is too tender for this world
you have always had overwhelming emotions
that were bigger than your body
you needed love and comfort
but no one had any to give to you

they did not want you to be
they tried to rob you of your tenderness
claiming the cruelty was *"toughening you up"*
but i refused
to turn into one of them
a shadow that moved through the world casting
shadows onto others

in this world
black women are not allowed to be soft
told from the youngest ages that we must be
strong
we have all of the strength
we carry the weight of responsibility
never able to escape accountability

and forced to have flexibility
while nursing others' fragility

we are taught to accommodate
care for others
not ourselves
but again i refuse
i am soft
and i am fragile
i am also strong
i will put myself first
in this world
that treats black women like we don't matter
in this world that does not allow us
to be us in peace

in all this i've learned
my sensitive heart
my ability to feel everything
is my gift
and it can never be taken away from me

growing tired

i am growing quite tired
of being the one who cares the most
growing tired
of being the one who loves the hardest
growing tired
of being the only one capable of honesty
growing tired

one day we're on the same page…
the next day we're not
but i wouldn't have thought
we were on the same page
if that was not
what i was told
why can't anyone just tell me
growing tired
lead with honesty
don't pretend to know me
stop walking in
to experience me
just to leave
at your earliest convenience
i'm growing tired
i know that i am something to be experienced
i am often taken for granted

and they often realize this once it is too late
i'm growing tired

i opened my heart to you
i thought that's what we were doing
now i stand here
heart in hands
so vulnerable
i'm growing tired
watching you walk away
and i suddenly wish i hadn't told you
anything
how you fill my heart up
my secrets
i want it back
i don't want you to know those things about me
so give them back
kindly forget them
those are things i tell to people i trust
and i do not trust you anymore

growing tired
of saying "but i thought"
i want it back
the love i shared
i wouldn't have dared
share those things with you
had i known what you were really thinking
the tiniest inkling

i wouldn't have let you see
me
i'm growing tired

look into my eyes as you hurt me
i won't make you feel better about doing this
i know you can see how my heart aches
i've never been good at hiding how i feel
i know you can see what you are doing to me
the reality we existed in
is now gone
instantly
what a loss this is
i enjoyed loving you
and as i grieve you
i wonder how i feel so deeply
i'll miss you
and
my heart will miss you
i'm growing tired
saying goodbye is
so hard
i'm tired

the box//searching

when i was a child
i boxed myself up
in the smallest box i could find
to keep myself safe

because i wasn't safe
i felt that all i had was me
so i hid me
tucked her away
so far away
where no one could get to her

so if i ever was safe
i could come out of hiding
but
i didn't know then
the things i'd have to face
to retrieve myself
from that very tiny box

there have been times
that i've been angry with myself
for getting in the box
because finding that box feels impossible
and it's maddening

it's like one second i know where it is…
sometimes i even have it in my hands
but then it's gone again
and another search begins

measuring happiness

what does happiness look like
for me
happiness appears when music makes my body
want to move
it appears when a hot cup of tea hits my soul just
right
it appears when i bask in the sunlight
and on a rainy day
when i am inspired
and
when i am spending quality time with myself
it appears when i interact with people i love
but
i don't feel happy all of the time
honestly most of the time i don't
most days are hard
and still
i don't think of it in a sense that it comes and
goes
happiness
i believe that it lies dormant
until you are ready to feel it

happiness isn't about feeling good all the time
or impossible expectations
it's not about having a good day
there's no need to pretend
it's about finding those moments throughout
your day
or week
where everything just makes sense
when you're just existing and your heart is so
full because of it
i relish in this feeling
it's about those tiny things that make you
grateful for waking up that day

everyone measures happiness differently
this is how i am choosing to measure mine
in a way that benefits me in my human
experience
how will you measure yours

grieving

there is so much of healing
that is grief
maybe all of it is

grieving other people
versions of them that don't exist anymore
the versions that once loved me
grieving the living
is
harder than grieving the dead

grieving things i missed out on in childhood
grieving what i lost then

grieving myself
the versions of me that only knew how to
survive
the versions of me that didn't know what real
love was
and the versions of me that caused harm to
myself because i didn't know any better
the version of me that thought i deserved the
abuse

grieving is such a fickle process

like growth, it's not at all linear
and also like growth
it takes strength
raw emotions are rarely easy to deal with

there are no guidelines for it
it's too easy to feel lost
you really have to figure out how to navigate in
a way that makes sense for you

stop comparing yourself
i know because i do it too
i desperately want to be healed
to be done crying
about the same things

but i know
i am forever changed
and that's okay
forcing it will only make me feel worse
i'm still learning to accept it
learning that i am enough
i am whole
i'm allowed to trust myself

and maybe the problem is that i'm trying to
make an impact in a way that someone else has
already made an impact instead of wanting to
make the impact only i could make